FAMOUS SHIPWRECKS
ATLANTIC OCEAN SHIPWRECKS

by Michelle Parkin

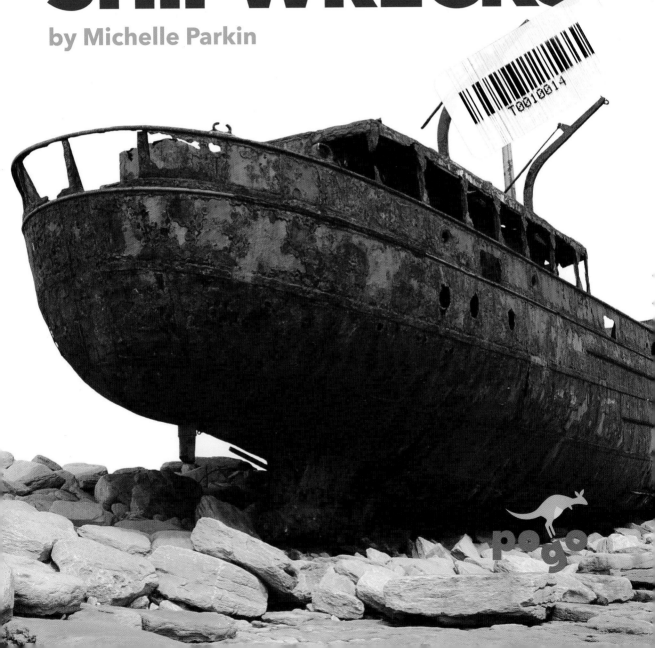

Ideas for Parents and Teachers

Pogo Books let children practice reading informational text while introducing them to nonfiction features such as headings, labels, sidebars, maps, and diagrams, as well as a table of contents, glossary, and index.

Carefully leveled text with a strong photo match offers early fluent readers the support they need to succeed.

Before Reading

- "Walk" through the book and point out the various nonfiction features. Ask the student what purpose each feature serves.
- Look at the glossary together. Read and discuss the words.

Read the Book

- Have the child read the book independently.
- Invite him or her to list questions that arise from reading.

After Reading

- Discuss the child's questions. Talk about how he or she might find answers to those questions.
- Prompt the child to think more. Ask: What are some reasons ships sink in the Atlantic Ocean? What can we learn from shipwrecks?

Pogo Books are published by Jump!
5357 Penn Avenue South
Minneapolis, MN 55419
www.jumplibrary.com

Library of Congress Cataloging-in-Publication Data

Names: Parkin, Michelle, 1984- author.
Title: Atlantic Ocean shipwrecks / by Michelle Parkin.
Description: Minneapolis, MN: Jump!, Inc., [2024]
Series: Famous shipwrecks | Includes index.
Audience: Ages 7-10
Identifiers: LCCN 2023030535 (print)
LCCN 2023030536 (ebook)
ISBN 9798889966593 (hardcover)
ISBN 9798889966609 (paperback)
ISBN 9798889966616 (ebook)
Subjects: LCSH: Shipwrecks–Atlantic Ocean–Juvenile literature. | Titanic (Steamship)–Juvenile literature. | Queen Anne's Revenge (Sailing vessel) –Juvenile literature.
Classification: LCC G525 P365 2024 (print)
LCC G525 (ebook)
DDC 910.9163–dc23/eng/20231002
LC record available at https://lccn.loc.gov/2023030535
LC ebook record available at https://lccn.loc.gov/2023030536

Editor: Alyssa Sorenson
Designer: Anna Peterson

Photo Credits: Ralph White/Getty, cover, 12-13; Gigi Peis/Shutterstock, 1; Dainer Salas/Shutterstock, 3; titoOnz/Shutterstock, 4; ESB Professional/Shutterstock, 5; Yandong Yang/Shutterstock, 6; US Coast Guard Photo/Alamy, 7; Joe Poe, Monitor National Marine Sanctuary advisory council/NOAA, 8-9; IanDagnall Computing/Alamy, 10-11; andrej67/iStock, 14-15; Archive PL/Alamy, 16-17; Eric Gevaert//Shutterstock, 18; ozgurkeser/iStock, 19; timsimages.uk/Shutterstock, 20-21; Laurent Gravier/iStock, 23.

Printed in the United States of America at Corporate Graphics in North Mankato, Minnesota.

TABLE OF CONTENTS

CHAPTER 1

WELCOME TO THE ATLANTIC

The Atlantic is the second-largest ocean. Only the Pacific is bigger. The Atlantic touches Europe and Africa in the east. It spreads to North and South America in the west. To its north is the Arctic Ocean. The Southern Ocean is south.

Atlantic
Ocean

Because the Atlantic is so large, different areas have different temperatures. The ocean is warm near **tropical** areas. It is cold enough for ice in others.

CHAPTER 2

WRECKED AT SEA

Traveling on the Atlantic Ocean is dangerous. Strong storms and **currents** tip ships over. **Icebergs** damage them. Many ships have sunk in the Atlantic Ocean.

iceberg ···▶

cannon ····▶

Queen Anne's Revenge was a pirate ship. In 1718, it was near North Carolina. It hit a **sandbar**. Water went into the ship. It sank.

The ship was found in 1996. It had many weapons. Some were cannons. Others were sword parts.

USS *Monitor*

The USS *Monitor* sailed during the U.S. Civil War (1861–1865). On December 29, 1862, a huge storm hit. Large waves and strong winds smashed against the ship. It started leaking. Soon, it sank.

In 1973, researchers found the **shipwreck**. It was near North Carolina. **Coral reefs** now grow on it. Fish use it as a home.

In April 1912, the RMS *Titanic* left England. It was sailing to New York City. More than 2,200 people were on the ship. There was ice in the northern Atlantic. *Titanic* hit a large iceberg. It tore holes in the ship.

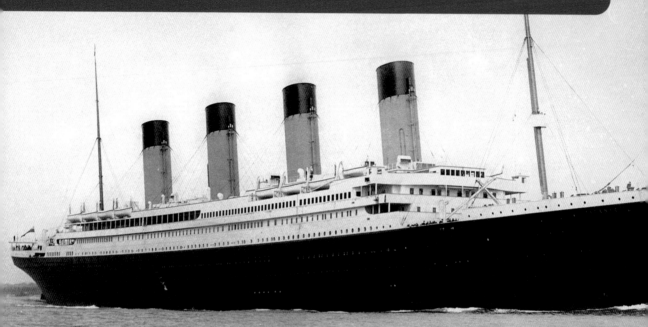

RMS *Titanic*

TAKE A LOOK!

How did *Titanic* sink? Take a look!

TITANIC HIT AN ICEBERG
It ripped holes in the side of the ship.

1

3

THE SHIP BROKE IN TWO
The front of the ship sank.
The back half soon followed.

2

WATER POURED IN
The front of the ship filled with water first. It was pulled down.

RMS *Titanic*

Titanic sank on April 15. There were not enough **lifeboats**. Many people were left in the freezing water. More than 1,500 people died.

The *Titanic* shipwreck was found in 1985. It rests about 12,500 feet (3,810 meters) below the surface. There have been many **expeditions** to see it.

DID YOU KNOW?

Some experts believe *Titanic* will be gone by 2050. Why? **Bacteria** are eating it.

In 1925, the SS *Cotopaxi* left South Carolina. There was a big storm. The ship disappeared.

In the 1980s, the shipwreck was found. It was near St. Augustine, Florida. But people did not know what ship it was. They figured it out in 2020.

WHAT DO YOU THINK?

For years, people thought *Cotopaxi* disappeared in the Bermuda Triangle. This is an area in the western Atlantic Ocean. Many people believe ships and planes mysteriously disappear here. Do you think the Bermuda Triangle is real?

SS *Andrea Doria*

It was July 25, 1956. The SS *Andrea Doria* was going to New York. It carried about 1,700 people. It was foggy outside. Another ship was nearby. It headed right toward *Andrea Doria*. The two ships hit each other.

The other ship did not sink. But water went into *Andrea Doria*. Fifty-one people died when it sank.

WHAT DO YOU THINK?

There were many reasons for the *Andrea Doria* disaster. It was hard to see in the fog. Both ships were moving fast. And the **crews** did not read their **radar** correctly. What could have been done to stop this disaster?

CHAPTER 3

SAILING THE ATLANTIC TODAY

People try to stay safe on the Atlantic. They look at ocean conditions. They are able to check currents and weather changes.

Ships still go missing. But today, **satellites** and radar can help find them.

radar

People look for shipwrecks. Some are military ships. Others belonged to pirates. Who knows what ship will be found next?

QUICK FACTS & TOOLS

WHERE THEY SANK IN THE ATLANTIC

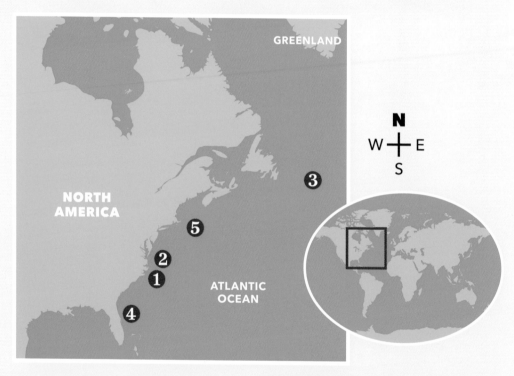

① *Queen Anne's Revenge* sank in 1718. It was discovered in 1996.

② The USS *Monitor* sank in 1862. Researchers found it in 1973.

③ The RMS *Titanic* set sail on April 10, 1912. It sank five days later after hitting an iceberg.

④ The SS *Cotopaxi* disappeared in 1925. The shipwreck was found in the 1980s.

⑤ On July 25, 1956, *Andrea Doria* hit another ship and sank beneath the ocean waves.

GLOSSARY

bacteria: Tiny living things found everywhere.

coral reefs: Long lines of coral that lie in warm, shallow waters.

crews: People who work on ships.

currents: Water that moves in a specific direction.

expeditions: Journeys taken by groups of people for a specific reason.

icebergs: Large pieces of ice that have broken off glaciers.

lifeboats: Boats on large ships that people use to get off the ships in emergencies.

radar: A system used to find aircraft, ships, and other objects by reflecting and receiving radio waves.

sandbar: A ridge of sand along an ocean's shore.

satellites: Objects placed in outer space to collect information or for communication.

shipwreck: The remains of a sunken ship.

tropical: Of or having to do with the hot, rainy area of the tropics.

INDEX

TO LEARN MORE

Finding more information is as easy as 1, 2, 3.

❶ **Go to www.factsurfer.com**

❷ **Enter "AtlanticOceanshipwrecks" into the search box.**

❸ **Choose your book to see a list of websites.**

FACT SURFER